LIFE
ULTIMATE PLANNER

October - December 2024

Q4

THIS PLANNER BELONGS TO

_____
NAME

_____
EMAIL

_____
CELL

GET STARTED

The Life Ultimate Planner is designed for anyone who wants to make their life count for more. It is a tool, a road map to be successful. The Life Ultimate Planner will help you create alignment with your life priorities. You will have increased confidence with decision making. You will find yourself in the drivers seat of life, feel organized and respected as an inspirational leader. It is the planner designed for people who love to plan, as well as those who need help planning. Start slow, set your own pace, but commit to it and watch your life become more manageable and productive.

Copyright©2024 Cheryl Jackson. All rights reserved.

ISBN: 978-1-960130-13-6

www.LiveLifeFullyCoaching.com

CONTENTS

2024 Calendar. 4
2025 Calendar. 5

October 2024 Calendar. 6
October Master Success Actions. 8
October Weekly and Daily Pages. 10
October Income Tracker. 60
October Expense Tracker 61
October Savings Tracker 62
October Monthly Progress. 63

November 2024 Calendar 64
November Master Success Actions. 66
November Weekly and Daily Pages 68
November Income Tracker 108
November Expense Tracker 109
November Savings Tracker 110
November Monthly Progress. 111

December 2024 Calendar 112
December Master Success Actions. 114
December Weekly and Daily Pages 116
December Income Tracker 166
December Expense Tracker 167
December Savings Tracker 168
December Monthly Progress. 169

Books to Read. 170
Wish List. 171
Website/App List. 172
Gifst List. 173
Notes Pages 174
Index 194

2024 CALENDAR

JANUARY

M	T	W	T	F	S	S
1	2	3	4	5	6	7
8	9	10	11	12	13	14
15	16	17	18	19	20	21
22	23	24	25	26	27	28
29	30	31				

FEBRUARY

M	T	W	T	F	S	S
			1	2	3	4
5	6	7	8	9	10	11
12	13	14	15	16	17	18
19	20	21	22	23	24	25
26	27	28	29			

MARCH

M	T	W	T	F	S	S
				1	2	3
4	5	6	7	8	9	10
11	12	13	14	15	16	17
18	19	20	21	22	23	24
25	26	27	28	29	30	31

APRIL

M	T	W	T	F	S	S
1	2	3	4	5	6	7
8	9	10	11	12	13	14
15	16	17	18	19	20	21
22	23	24	25	26	27	28
29	30					

MAY

M	T	W	T	F	S	S
		1	2	3	4	5
6	7	8	9	10	11	12
13	14	15	16	17	18	19
20	21	22	23	24	25	26
27	28	29	30	31		

JUNE

M	T	W	T	F	S	S
					1	2
3	4	5	6	7	8	9
10	11	12	13	14	15	16
17	18	19	20	21	22	23
24	25	26	27	28	29	30

JULY

M	T	W	T	F	S	S
1	2	3	4	5	6	7
8	9	10	11	12	13	14
15	16	17	18	19	20	21
22	23	24	25	26	27	28
29	30	31				

AUGUST

M	T	W	T	F	S	S
			1	2	3	4
5	6	7	8	9	10	11
12	13	14	15	16	17	18
19	20	21	22	23	24	25
26	27	28	29	30	31	

SEPTEMBER

M	T	W	T	F	S	S
						1
2	3	4	5	6	7	8
9	10	11	12	13	14	15
16	17	18	19	20	21	22
23	24	25	26	27	28	29
30						

OCTOBER

M	T	W	T	F	S	S
	1	2	3	4	5	6
7	8	9	10	11	12	13
14	15	16	17	18	19	20
21	22	23	24	25	26	27
28	29	30	31			

NOVEMBER

M	T	W	T	F	S	S
				1	2	3
4	5	6	7	8	9	10
11	12	13	14	15	16	17
18	19	20	21	22	23	24
25	26	27	28	29	30	

DECEMBER

M	T	W	T	F	S	S
						1
2	3	4	5	6	7	8
9	10	11	12	13	14	15
16	17	18	19	20	21	22
23	24	25	26	27	28	29
30	31					

2025 CALENDAR

JANUARY

M	T	W	T	F	S	S
		1	2	3	4	5
6	7	8	9	10	11	12
13	14	15	16	17	18	19
20	21	22	23	24	25	26
27	28	29	30	31		

FEBRUARY

M	T	W	T	F	S	S
					1	2
3	4	5	6	7	8	9
10	11	12	13	14	15	16
17	18	19	20	21	22	23
24	25	26	27	28		

MARCH

M	T	W	T	F	S	S
					1	2
3	4	5	6	7	8	9
10	11	12	13	14	15	16
17	18	19	20	21	22	23
24	25	26	27	28	29	30
31						

APRIL

M	T	W	T	F	S	S
	1	2	3	4	5	6
7	8	9	10	11	12	13
14	15	16	17	18	19	20
21	22	23	24	25	26	27
28	29	30				

MAY

M	T	W	T	F	S	S
			1	2	3	4
5	6	7	8	9	10	11
12	13	14	15	16	17	18
19	20	21	22	23	24	25
26	27	28	29	30	31	

JUNE

M	T	W	T	F	S	S
						1
2	3	4	5	6	7	8
9	10	11	12	13	14	15
16	17	18	19	20	21	22
23	24	25	26	27	28	29
30						

JULY

M	T	W	T	F	S	S
	1	2	3	4	5	6
7	8	9	10	11	12	13
14	15	16	17	18	19	20
21	22	23	24	25	26	27
28	29	30	31			

AUGUST

M	T	W	T	F	S	S
				1	2	3
4	5	6	7	8	9	10
11	12	13	14	15	16	17
18	19	20	21	22	23	24
25	26	27	28	29	30	31

SEPTEMBER

M	T	W	T	F	S	S
1	2	3	4	5	6	7
8	9	10	11	12	13	14
15	16	17	18	19	20	21
22	23	24	25	26	27	28
29	30					

OCTOBER

M	T	W	T	F	S	S
		1	2	3	4	5
6	7	8	9	10	11	12
13	14	15	16	17	18	19
20	21	22	23	24	25	26
27	28	29	30	31		

NOVEMBER

M	T	W	T	F	S	S
					1	2
3	4	5	6	7	8	9
10	11	12	13	14	15	16
17	18	19	20	21	22	23
24	25	26	27	28	29	30

DECEMBER

M	T	W	T	F	S	S
1	2	3	4	5	6	7
8	9	10	11	12	13	14
15	16	17	18	19	20	21
22	23	24	25	26	27	28
29	30	31				

OCTOBER

MONDAY	TUESDAY	WEDNESDAY	THURSDAY
	1	2	3
7	8	9	10
14	15	16	17
21	22	23	24
28	29	30	31

GOALS

2024

FRIDAY	SATURDAY	SUNDAY	NOTES
4	5	6	
11	12	13	
18	19	20	
25	26	27	

NOTES

MASTER SUCCESS ACTIONS
OCTOBER 2024

List 4 life areas and your goals to focus on this month:

1.

2.

3.

4.

Use this master task list for the big action steps you will commit to do this month. They will accomplish the goals you set to improve your life in the 4 areas of focus. Your daily tasks will be the small steps to accomplish these bigger steps.

DONE	SUCCESS ACTIONS

NOTES

WEEKLY PLANNER

QUOTE OF THE WEEK:

MONDAY
30

TUESDAY
1

WEDNESDAY
2

THURSDAY
3

FRIDAY
4

SATURDAY
5

SUNDAY
6

PRIORITIES / GOALS

○
○
○
○
○
○
○
○
○

NOTES

SUCCESS FOCUS:

SEPTEMBER 30 - OCTOBER 6, 2024

	BREAKFAST	LUNCH	DINNER	SNACKS
M				
T				
W				
T				
F				
S				
S				

SHOPPING LIST:

NOTES

MONDAY
SEPTEMBER 2024   **30**

TODAY'S PRAYER & FOCUS:

SCHEDULE

TIME	APPOINTMENT

PRIORITIES / GOALS

- ◯
- ◯
- ◯
- ◯
- ◯
- ◯
- ◯
- ◯
- ◯
- ◯

NOTES & SCRIBBLES

HABITS – 1 NEW PER MONTH
1.
2.
3.

TODAY I'M GRATEFUL FOR

1

TUESDAY
OCTOBER 2024

TODAY'S PRAYER & FOCUS:

SCHEDULE

TIME	APPOINTMENT

PRIORITIES / GOALS

- ○
- ○
- ○
- ○
- ○
- ○
- ○
- ○
- ○
- ○

NOTES & SCRIBBLES

HABITS – 1 NEW PER MONTH

1.
2.
3.

TODAY I'M GRATEFUL FOR

WEDNESDAY
OCTOBER 2024

2

TODAY'S PRAYER & FOCUS:

SCHEDULE

TIME	APPOINTMENT

PRIORITIES / GOALS

- ○
- ○
- ○
- ○
- ○
- ○
- ○
- ○
- ○
- ○

NOTES & SCRIBBLES

HABITS – 1 NEW PER MONTH
1.
2.
3.

TODAY I'M GRATEFUL FOR

3

THURSDAY
OCTOBER 2024

TODAY'S PRAYER & FOCUS:

SCHEDULE

TIME	APPOINTMENT

PRIORITIES / GOALS

- ○
- ○
- ○
- ○
- ○
- ○
- ○
- ○
- ○
- ○

NOTES & SCRIBBLES

HABITS – 1 NEW PER MONTH

1.
2.
3.

TODAY I'M GRATEFUL FOR

FRIDAY
OCTOBER 2024

4

TODAY'S PRAYER & FOCUS:

SCHEDULE

TIME	APPOINTMENT

PRIORITIES / GOALS

- ○
- ○
- ○
- ○
- ○
- ○
- ○
- ○
- ○

NOTES & SCRIBBLES

HABITS – 1 NEW PER MONTH
1.
2.
3.

TODAY I'M GRATEFUL FOR

5

SATURDAY
OCTOBER 2024

TODAY'S PRAYER & FOCUS:

SCHEDULE

TIME	APPOINTMENT

PRIORITIES / GOALS

- ○
- ○
- ○
- ○
- ○
- ○
- ○
- ○
- ○

NOTES & SCRIBBLES

HABITS — 1 NEW PER MONTH

1.
2.
3.

TODAY I'M GRATEFUL FOR

SUNDAY
OCTOBER 2024

6

TODAY'S PRAYER & FOCUS:

SCHEDULE

TIME	APPOINTMENT

PRIORITIES / GOALS

- ○
- ○
- ○
- ○
- ○
- ○
- ○
- ○
- ○

NOTES & SCRIBBLES

HABITS – 1 NEW PER MONTH
1.
2.
3.

TODAY I'M GRATEFUL FOR

WEEKLY PLANNER

QUOTE OF THE WEEK:

MONDAY 7	
TUESDAY 8	
WEDNESDAY 9	
THURSDAY 10	
FRIDAY 11	
SATURDAY 12	
SUNDAY 13	

PRIORITIES / GOALS

○
○
○
○
○
○
○
○
○
○

NOTES

SUCCESS FOCUS:

OCTOBER 7 – 13, 2024

	BREAKFAST	LUNCH	DINNER	SNACKS
M				
T				
W				
T				
F				
S				
S				

SHOPPING LIST:

NOTES

MONDAY
OCTOBER 2024

7

TODAY'S PRAYER & FOCUS:

SCHEDULE

TIME	APPOINTMENT

PRIORITIES / GOALS

- ◯
- ◯
- ◯
- ◯
- ◯
- ◯
- ◯
- ◯
- ◯
- ◯

NOTES & SCRIBBLES

HABITS — 1 NEW PER MONTH

1.
2.
3.

TODAY I'M GRATEFUL FOR

8

TUESDAY
OCTOBER 2024

TODAY'S PRAYER & FOCUS:

SCHEDULE

TIME	APPOINTMENT

PRIORITIES / GOALS

- ◯
- ◯
- ◯
- ◯
- ◯
- ◯
- ◯
- ◯
- ◯

NOTES & SCRIBBLES

HABITS – 1 NEW PER MONTH

1.
2.
3.

TODAY I'M GRATEFUL FOR

WEDNESDAY
OCTOBER 2024

9

TODAY'S PRAYER & FOCUS:

SCHEDULE

TIME	APPOINTMENT

PRIORITIES / GOALS

- ○
- ○
- ○
- ○
- ○
- ○
- ○
- ○
- ○
- ○

NOTES & SCRIBBLES

HABITS – 1 NEW PER MONTH
1.
2.
3.

TODAY I'M GRATEFUL FOR

10

THURSDAY
OCTOBER 2024

TODAY'S PRAYER & FOCUS:

SCHEDULE

TIME	APPOINTMENT

PRIORITIES / GOALS

○
○
○
○
○
○
○
○
○
○

NOTES & SCRIBBLES

HABITS – 1 NEW PER MONTH

1.
2.
3.

TODAY I'M GRATEFUL FOR

FRIDAY
OCTOBER 2024
11

TODAY'S PRAYER & FOCUS:

SCHEDULE

TIME	APPOINTMENT

PRIORITIES / GOALS

- ○
- ○
- ○
- ○
- ○
- ○
- ○
- ○
- ○

NOTES & SCRIBBLES

HABITS – 1 NEW PER MONTH
1.
2.
3.

TODAY I'M GRATEFUL FOR

12
SATURDAY
OCTOBER 2024

TODAY'S PRAYER & FOCUS:

SCHEDULE

TIME	APPOINTMENT

PRIORITIES / GOALS

- ○
- ○
- ○
- ○
- ○
- ○
- ○
- ○
- ○
- ○

NOTES & SCRIBBLES

HABITS – 1 NEW PER MONTH
1.
2.
3.

TODAY I'M GRATEFUL FOR

SUNDAY
OCTOBER 2024

13

TODAY'S PRAYER & FOCUS:

SCHEDULE

TIME	APPOINTMENT

PRIORITIES / GOALS

- ◯
- ◯
- ◯
- ◯
- ◯
- ◯
- ◯
- ◯
- ◯

NOTES & SCRIBBLES

HABITS – 1 NEW PER MONTH

1.
2.
3.

TODAY I'M GRATEFUL FOR

WEEKLY PLANNER

QUOTE OF THE WEEK:

MONDAY
14

TUESDAY
15

WEDNESDAY
16

THURSDAY
17

FRIDAY
18

SATURDAY
19

SUNDAY
20

SUCCESS FOCUS:

PRIORITIES / GOALS

-
-
-
-
-
-
-
-
-
-

NOTES

OCTOBER 14 – 20, 2024

	BREAKFAST	LUNCH	DINNER	SNACKS
M				
T				
W				
T				
F				
S				
S				

SHOPPING LIST:

NOTES

MONDAY
OCTOBER 2024 — 14

TODAY'S PRAYER & FOCUS:

SCHEDULE

TIME	APPOINTMENT

PRIORITIES / GOALS

- ○
- ○
- ○
- ○
- ○
- ○
- ○
- ○
- ○

NOTES & SCRIBBLES

HABITS – 1 NEW PER MONTH
1.
2.
3.

TODAY I'M GRATEFUL FOR

15

TUESDAY
OCTOBER 2024

TODAY'S PRAYER & FOCUS:

SCHEDULE

TIME	APPOINTMENT

PRIORITIES / GOALS

- ○
- ○
- ○
- ○
- ○
- ○
- ○
- ○
- ○
- ○

NOTES & SCRIBBLES

HABITS – 1 NEW PER MONTH

1.
2.
3.

TODAY I'M GRATEFUL FOR

WEDNESDAY
OCTOBER 2024

16

TODAY'S PRAYER & FOCUS:

SCHEDULE

TIME	APPOINTMENT

PRIORITIES / GOALS

- ◯
- ◯
- ◯
- ◯
- ◯
- ◯
- ◯
- ◯
- ◯

NOTES & SCRIBBLES

HABITS – 1 NEW PER MONTH

1.
2.
3.

TODAY I'M GRATEFUL FOR

17

THURSDAY
OCTOBER 2024

TODAY'S PRAYER & FOCUS:

SCHEDULE

TIME	APPOINTMENT

PRIORITIES / GOALS

- ○
- ○
- ○
- ○
- ○
- ○
- ○
- ○
- ○
- ○

NOTES & SCRIBBLES

HABITS – 1 NEW PER MONTH
1.
2.
3.

TODAY I'M GRATEFUL FOR

FRIDAY
OCTOBER 2024
18

TODAY'S PRAYER & FOCUS:

SCHEDULE

TIME	APPOINTMENT

PRIORITIES / GOALS

- ◯
- ◯
- ◯
- ◯
- ◯
- ◯
- ◯
- ◯
- ◯

NOTES & SCRIBBLES

HABITS – 1 NEW PER MONTH

1.
2.
3.

TODAY I'M GRATEFUL FOR

19

SATURDAY
OCTOBER 2024

TODAY'S PRAYER & FOCUS:

SCHEDULE

TIME	APPOINTMENT

PRIORITIES / GOALS

- ○
- ○
- ○
- ○
- ○
- ○
- ○
- ○
- ○
- ○

NOTES & SCRIBBLES

HABITS – 1 NEW PER MONTH

1.
2.
3.

TODAY I'M GRATEFUL FOR

SUNDAY
OCTOBER 2024   **20**

TODAY'S PRAYER & FOCUS:

SCHEDULE

TIME	APPOINTMENT

PRIORITIES / GOALS

- ◯
- ◯
- ◯
- ◯
- ◯
- ◯
- ◯
- ◯
- ◯
- ◯

NOTES & SCRIBBLES

HABITS – 1 NEW PER MONTH

1.
2.
3.

TODAY I'M GRATEFUL FOR

WEEKLY PLANNER

QUOTE OF THE WEEK:

MONDAY 21
TUESDAY 22
WEDNESDAY 23
THURSDAY 24
FRIDAY 25
SATURDAY 26
SUNDAY 27

SUCCESS FOCUS:

PRIORITIES / GOALS

○
○
○
○
○
○
○
○
○
○

NOTES

OCTOBER 21 – 27, 2024

	BREAKFAST	LUNCH	DINNER	SNACKS
M				
T				
W				
T				
F				
S				
S				

SHOPPING LIST:

NOTES

MONDAY
OCTOBER 2024 — 21

TODAY'S PRAYER & FOCUS:

SCHEDULE

TIME	APPOINTMENT

PRIORITIES / GOALS

- ○
- ○
- ○
- ○
- ○
- ○
- ○
- ○
- ○
- ○

NOTES & SCRIBBLES

HABITS – 1 NEW PER MONTH

1.
2.
3.

TODAY I'M GRATEFUL FOR

22
TUESDAY
OCTOBER 2024

TODAY'S PRAYER & FOCUS:

SCHEDULE

TIME	APPOINTMENT

PRIORITIES / GOALS

- ○
- ○
- ○
- ○
- ○
- ○
- ○
- ○
- ○
- ○

NOTES & SCRIBBLES

HABITS — 1 NEW PER MONTH

1.
2.
3.

TODAY I'M GRATEFUL FOR

WEDNESDAY
OCTOBER 2024
23

TODAY'S PRAYER & FOCUS:

SCHEDULE

TIME	APPOINTMENT

PRIORITIES / GOALS

- ◯
- ◯
- ◯
- ◯
- ◯
- ◯
- ◯
- ◯
- ◯
- ◯

NOTES & SCRIBBLES

HABITS – 1 NEW PER MONTH
1.
2.
3.

TODAY I'M GRATEFUL FOR

24

THURSDAY
OCTOBER 2024

TODAY'S PRAYER & FOCUS:

SCHEDULE

TIME	APPOINTMENT

PRIORITIES / GOALS

- ○
- ○
- ○
- ○
- ○
- ○
- ○
- ○
- ○
- ○

NOTES & SCRIBBLES

HABITS – 1 NEW PER MONTH

1.
2.
3.

TODAY I'M GRATEFUL FOR

FRIDAY
OCTOBER 2024   **25**

TODAY'S PRAYER & FOCUS:

SCHEDULE

TIME	APPOINTMENT

PRIORITIES / GOALS

- ○
- ○
- ○
- ○
- ○
- ○
- ○
- ○
- ○

NOTES & SCRIBBLES

HABITS – 1 NEW PER MONTH
1.
2.
3.

TODAY I'M GRATEFUL FOR

26 SATURDAY
OCTOBER 2024

TODAY'S PRAYER & FOCUS:

SCHEDULE

TIME	APPOINTMENT

PRIORITIES / GOALS

- ○
- ○
- ○
- ○
- ○
- ○
- ○
- ○
- ○
- ○

NOTES & SCRIBBLES

HABITS – 1 NEW PER MONTH
1.
2.
3.

TODAY I'M GRATEFUL FOR

SUNDAY
OCTOBER 2024 **27**

TODAY'S PRAYER & FOCUS:

SCHEDULE

TIME	APPOINTMENT

PRIORITIES / GOALS

- ◯
- ◯
- ◯
- ◯
- ◯
- ◯
- ◯
- ◯
- ◯
- ◯

NOTES & SCRIBBLES

HABITS – 1 NEW PER MONTH
1.
2.
3.

TODAY I'M GRATEFUL FOR

WEEKLY PLANNER

QUOTE OF THE WEEK:

MONDAY 28
TUESDAY 29
WEDNESDAY 30
THURSDAY 31
FRIDAY 1
SATURDAY 2
SUNDAY 3

PRIORITIES / GOALS

- ○
- ○
- ○
- ○
- ○
- ○
- ○
- ○
- ○
- ○

NOTES

SUCCESS FOCUS:

OCTOBER 28 – NOVEMBER 3, 2024

	BREAKFAST	LUNCH	DINNER	SNACKS
M				
T				
W				
T				
F				
S				
S				

SHOPPING LIST:

NOTES

MONDAY
OCTOBER 2024
28

TODAY'S PRAYER & FOCUS:

SCHEDULE

TIME	APPOINTMENT

PRIORITIES / GOALS

○
○
○
○
○
○
○
○
○
○

NOTES & SCRIBBLES

HABITS – 1 NEW PER MONTH
1.
2.
3.

TODAY I'M GRATEFUL FOR

29

TUESDAY
OCTOBER 2024

TODAY'S PRAYER & FOCUS:

SCHEDULE

TIME	APPOINTMENT

PRIORITIES / GOALS

- ○
- ○
- ○
- ○
- ○
- ○
- ○
- ○
- ○
- ○

NOTES & SCRIBBLES

HABITS – 1 NEW PER MONTH

1.
2.
3.

TODAY I'M GRATEFUL FOR

WEDNESDAY
OCTOBER 2024 **30**

TODAY'S PRAYER & FOCUS:

SCHEDULE

TIME	APPOINTMENT

PRIORITIES / GOALS

- ○
- ○
- ○
- ○
- ○
- ○
- ○
- ○
- ○

NOTES & SCRIBBLES

HABITS – 1 NEW PER MONTH
1.
2.
3.

TODAY I'M GRATEFUL FOR

31

THURSDAY
OCTOBER 2024

TODAY'S PRAYER & FOCUS:

SCHEDULE

TIME	APPOINTMENT

PRIORITIES / GOALS

- ○
- ○
- ○
- ○
- ○
- ○
- ○
- ○
- ○

NOTES & SCRIBBLES

HABITS – 1 NEW PER MONTH

1.
2.
3.

TODAY I'M GRATEFUL FOR

FRIDAY
NOVEMBER 2024 — 1

TODAY'S PRAYER & FOCUS:

SCHEDULE

TIME	APPOINTMENT

PRIORITIES / GOALS

- ○
- ○
- ○
- ○
- ○
- ○
- ○
- ○
- ○
- ○

NOTES & SCRIBBLES

HABITS – 1 NEW PER MONTH

1.
2.
3.

TODAY I'M GRATEFUL FOR

2

SATURDAY
NOVEMBER 2024

TODAY'S PRAYER & FOCUS:

SCHEDULE

TIME	APPOINTMENT

PRIORITIES / GOALS

- ○
- ○
- ○
- ○
- ○
- ○
- ○
- ○
- ○
- ○

NOTES & SCRIBBLES

HABITS – 1 NEW PER MONTH
1.
2.
3.

TODAY I'M GRATEFUL FOR

SUNDAY
NOVEMBER 2024

3

TODAY'S PRAYER & FOCUS:

SCHEDULE

TIME	APPOINTMENT

PRIORITIES / GOALS

- ○
- ○
- ○
- ○
- ○
- ○
- ○
- ○
- ○

NOTES & SCRIBBLES

HABITS – 1 NEW PER MONTH
1.
2.
3.

TODAY I'M GRATEFUL FOR

OCTOBER 2024 INCOME TRACKER

DATE	INCOME	CATEGORY	AMOUNT
TOTAL			

OCTOBER 2024 EXPENSE TRACKER

DATE	EXPENSE	CATEGORY	AMOUNT
TOTAL			

OCTOBER 2024 SAVINGS TRACKER

SAVING FOR: _____   GOAL AMOUNT: _____

DATE	NOTES	AMOUNT	BALANCE
TOTAL			

MONTHLY PROGRESS - OCTOBER 2024

I HAVE ACHIEVED...

I AM THANKFUL...

I'D LIKE TO IMPROVE...

HOW I WILL CELEBRATE WHAT I DID WELL...

NOVEMBER

MONDAY	TUESDAY	WEDNESDAY	THURSDAY
4	5	6	7
11	12	13	14
18	19	20	21
25	26	27	28

GOALS

2024

FRIDAY	SATURDAY	SUNDAY	NOTES
1	2	3	
8	9	10	
15	16	17	
22	23	24	
29	30	1	

NOTES

MASTER SUCCESS ACTIONS
NOVEMBER 2024

List 4 life areas and your goals to focus on this month:

1.

2.

3.

4.

Use this master task list for the big action steps you will commit to do this month. They will accomplish the goals you set to improve your life in the 4 areas of focus. Your daily tasks will be the small steps to accomplish these bigger steps.

DONE	SUCCESS ACTIONS

NOTES

WEEKLY PLANNER

QUOTE OF THE WEEK:

MONDAY
4

TUESDAY
5

WEDNESDAY
6

THURSDAY
7

FRIDAY
8

SATURDAY
9

SUNDAY
10

SUCCESS FOCUS:

PRIORITIES / GOALS

- ◯
- ◯
- ◯
- ◯
- ◯
- ◯
- ◯
- ◯
- ◯
- ◯

NOTES

NOVEMBER 4 – 10, 2024

	BREAKFAST	LUNCH	DINNER	SNACKS
M				
T				
W				
T				
F				
S				
S				

SHOPPING LIST:

NOTES

MONDAY
NOVEMBER 2024

4

TODAY'S PRAYER & FOCUS:

SCHEDULE

TIME	APPOINTMENT

PRIORITIES / GOALS

- ○
- ○
- ○
- ○
- ○
- ○
- ○
- ○
- ○
- ○

NOTES & SCRIBBLES

HABITS – 1 NEW PER MONTH
1.
2.
3.

TODAY I'M GRATEFUL FOR

5
TUESDAY
NOVEMBER 2024

TODAY'S PRAYER & FOCUS:

SCHEDULE

TIME	APPOINTMENT

PRIORITIES / GOALS

- ○
- ○
- ○
- ○
- ○
- ○
- ○
- ○
- ○
- ○

NOTES & SCRIBBLES

HABITS – 1 NEW PER MONTH

1.
2.
3.

TODAY I'M GRATEFUL FOR

WEDNESDAY
NOVEMBER 2024

6

TODAY'S PRAYER & FOCUS:

SCHEDULE

TIME	APPOINTMENT

PRIORITIES / GOALS

- ○
- ○
- ○
- ○
- ○
- ○
- ○
- ○
- ○
- ○

NOTES & SCRIBBLES

HABITS – 1 NEW PER MONTH
1.
2.
3.

TODAY I'M GRATEFUL FOR

7

THURSDAY
NOVEMBER 2024

TODAY'S PRAYER & FOCUS:

SCHEDULE

TIME	APPOINTMENT

PRIORITIES / GOALS

- ○
- ○
- ○
- ○
- ○
- ○
- ○
- ○
- ○
- ○

NOTES & SCRIBBLES

HABITS – 1 NEW PER MONTH

1.
2.
3.

TODAY I'M GRATEFUL FOR

FRIDAY
NOVEMBER 2024

8

TODAY'S PRAYER & FOCUS:

SCHEDULE

TIME	APPOINTMENT

PRIORITIES / GOALS

- ◯
- ◯
- ◯
- ◯
- ◯
- ◯
- ◯
- ◯
- ◯

NOTES & SCRIBBLES

HABITS – 1 NEW PER MONTH

1.
2.
3.

TODAY I'M GRATEFUL FOR

9

SATURDAY
NOVEMBER 2024

TODAY'S PRAYER & FOCUS:

SCHEDULE

TIME	APPOINTMENT

PRIORITIES / GOALS

- ○
- ○
- ○
- ○
- ○
- ○
- ○
- ○
- ○
- ○

NOTES & SCRIBBLES

HABITS – 1 NEW PER MONTH

1.
2.
3.

TODAY I'M GRATEFUL FOR

SUNDAY
NOVEMBER 2024 **10**

TODAY'S PRAYER & FOCUS:

SCHEDULE

TIME	APPOINTMENT

PRIORITIES / GOALS

- ○
- ○
- ○
- ○
- ○
- ○
- ○
- ○
- ○

NOTES & SCRIBBLES

HABITS – 1 NEW PER MONTH
1.
2.
3.

TODAY I'M GRATEFUL FOR

WEEKLY PLANNER

QUOTE OF THE WEEK:

| MONDAY |
| 11 |

| TUESDAY |
| 12 |

| WEDNESDAY |
| 13 |

| THURSDAY |
| 14 |

| FRIDAY |
| 15 |

| SATURDAY |
| 16 |

| SUNDAY |
| 17 |

PRIORITIES / GOALS

○
○
○
○
○
○
○
○
○
○

NOTES

SUCCESS FOCUS:

NOVEMBER 11 – 17, 2024

	BREAKFAST	LUNCH	DINNER	SNACKS
M				
T				
W				
T				
F				
S				
S				

SHOPPING LIST:

NOTES

MONDAY
NOVEMBER 2024

11

TODAY'S PRAYER & FOCUS:

SCHEDULE

TIME	APPOINTMENT

PRIORITIES / GOALS

- ◯
- ◯
- ◯
- ◯
- ◯
- ◯
- ◯
- ◯
- ◯
- ◯

NOTES & SCRIBBLES

HABITS – 1 NEW PER MONTH

1.
2.
3.

TODAY I'M GRATEFUL FOR

12 TUESDAY
NOVEMBER 2024

TODAY'S PRAYER & FOCUS:

SCHEDULE

TIME	APPOINTMENT

PRIORITIES / GOALS

- ○
- ○
- ○
- ○
- ○
- ○
- ○
- ○
- ○

NOTES & SCRIBBLES

HABITS – 1 NEW PER MONTH
1.
2.
3.

TODAY I'M GRATEFUL FOR

WEDNESDAY
NOVEMBER 2024
13

TODAY'S PRAYER & FOCUS:

SCHEDULE

TIME	APPOINTMENT

PRIORITIES / GOALS

○
○
○
○
○
○
○
○
○
○

NOTES & SCRIBBLES

HABITS – 1 NEW PER MONTH

1.
2.
3.

TODAY I'M GRATEFUL FOR

14

THURSDAY
NOVEMBER 2024

TODAY'S PRAYER & FOCUS:

SCHEDULE

TIME	APPOINTMENT

PRIORITIES / GOALS

- ○
- ○
- ○
- ○
- ○
- ○
- ○
- ○
- ○

NOTES & SCRIBBLES

HABITS – 1 NEW PER MONTH

1.
2.
3.

TODAY I'M GRATEFUL FOR

FRIDAY
NOVEMBER 2024
15

TODAY'S PRAYER & FOCUS:

SCHEDULE

TIME	APPOINTMENT

PRIORITIES / GOALS

- ◯
- ◯
- ◯
- ◯
- ◯
- ◯
- ◯
- ◯
- ◯
- ◯

NOTES & SCRIBBLES

HABITS – 1 NEW PER MONTH

1.
2.
3.

TODAY I'M GRATEFUL FOR

16

SATURDAY
NOVEMBER 2024

TODAY'S PRAYER & FOCUS:

SCHEDULE

TIME	APPOINTMENT

PRIORITIES / GOALS

○
○
○
○
○
○
○
○
○
○

NOTES & SCRIBBLES

HABITS – 1 NEW PER MONTH

1.
2.
3.

TODAY I'M GRATEFUL FOR

SUNDAY
NOVEMBER 2024   **17**

TODAY'S PRAYER & FOCUS:

SCHEDULE

TIME	APPOINTMENT

PRIORITIES / GOALS

- ◯
- ◯
- ◯
- ◯
- ◯
- ◯
- ◯
- ◯
- ◯
- ◯

NOTES & SCRIBBLES

HABITS – 1 NEW PER MONTH
1.
2.
3.

TODAY I'M GRATEFUL FOR

WEEKLY PLANNER

QUOTE OF THE WEEK:

MONDAY 18

TUESDAY 19

WEDNESDAY 20

THURSDAY 21

FRIDAY 22

SATURDAY 23

SUNDAY 24

PRIORITIES / GOALS

- ○
- ○
- ○
- ○
- ○
- ○
- ○
- ○
- ○
- ○

NOTES

SUCCESS FOCUS:

NOVEMBER 18 – 24, 2024

	BREAKFAST	LUNCH	DINNER	SNACKS
M				
T				
W				
T				
F				
S				
S				

SHOPPING LIST:

NOTES

MONDAY
NOVEMBER 2024 — **18**

TODAY'S PRAYER & FOCUS:

SCHEDULE

TIME	APPOINTMENT

PRIORITIES / GOALS

- ◯
- ◯
- ◯
- ◯
- ◯
- ◯
- ◯
- ◯
- ◯

NOTES & SCRIBBLES

HABITS – 1 NEW PER MONTH
1.
2.
3.

TODAY I'M GRATEFUL FOR

19

TUESDAY
NOVEMBER 2024

TODAY'S PRAYER & FOCUS:

SCHEDULE

TIME	APPOINTMENT

PRIORITIES / GOALS

- ○
- ○
- ○
- ○
- ○
- ○
- ○
- ○
- ○

NOTES & SCRIBBLES

HABITS – 1 NEW PER MONTH

1.
2.
3.

TODAY I'M GRATEFUL FOR

WEDNESDAY
NOVEMBER 2024 **20**

TODAY'S PRAYER & FOCUS:

SCHEDULE

TIME	APPOINTMENT

PRIORITIES / GOALS

- ○
- ○
- ○
- ○
- ○
- ○
- ○
- ○
- ○
- ○

NOTES & SCRIBBLES

HABITS – 1 NEW PER MONTH
1.
2.
3.

TODAY I'M GRATEFUL FOR

21 THURSDAY
NOVEMBER 2024

TODAY'S PRAYER & FOCUS:

SCHEDULE

TIME	APPOINTMENT

PRIORITIES / GOALS

- ○
- ○
- ○
- ○
- ○
- ○
- ○
- ○
- ○
- ○

NOTES & SCRIBBLES

HABITS – 1 NEW PER MONTH

1.
2.
3.

TODAY I'M GRATEFUL FOR

FRIDAY
NOVEMBER 2024
22

TODAY'S PRAYER & FOCUS:

SCHEDULE

TIME	APPOINTMENT

PRIORITIES / GOALS

- ◯
- ◯
- ◯
- ◯
- ◯
- ◯
- ◯
- ◯
- ◯
- ◯

NOTES & SCRIBBLES

HABITS – 1 NEW PER MONTH
1.
2.
3.

TODAY I'M GRATEFUL FOR

23
SATURDAY
NOVEMBER 2024

TODAY'S PRAYER & FOCUS:

SCHEDULE

TIME	APPOINTMENT

PRIORITIES / GOALS

- ○
- ○
- ○
- ○
- ○
- ○
- ○
- ○
- ○
- ○

NOTES & SCRIBBLES

HABITS – 1 NEW PER MONTH

1.
2.
3.

TODAY I'M GRATEFUL FOR

SUNDAY
NOVEMBER 2024 — 24

TODAY'S PRAYER & FOCUS:

SCHEDULE

TIME	APPOINTMENT

PRIORITIES / GOALS

- ○
- ○
- ○
- ○
- ○
- ○
- ○
- ○
- ○

NOTES & SCRIBBLES

HABITS – 1 NEW PER MONTH
1.
2.
3.

TODAY I'M GRATEFUL FOR

WEEKLY PLANNER

QUOTE OF THE WEEK:

MONDAY
25

TUESDAY
26

WEDNESDAY
27

THURSDAY
28

FRIDAY
29

SATURDAY
30

SUNDAY
1

SUCCESS FOCUS:

PRIORITIES / GOALS

- ○
- ○
- ○
- ○
- ○
- ○
- ○
- ○
- ○
- ○

NOTES

NOVEMBER 25 – DECEMBER 1, 2024

	BREAKFAST	LUNCH	DINNER	SNACKS
M				
T				
W				
T				
F				
S				
S				

SHOPPING LIST:

NOTES

MONDAY
NOVEMBER 2024 **25**

TODAY'S PRAYER & FOCUS:

SCHEDULE

TIME	APPOINTMENT

PRIORITIES / GOALS

- ○
- ○
- ○
- ○
- ○
- ○
- ○
- ○
- ○
- ○

NOTES & SCRIBBLES

HABITS – 1 NEW PER MONTH

1.
2.
3.

TODAY I'M GRATEFUL FOR

26 TUESDAY
NOVEMBER 2024

TODAY'S PRAYER & FOCUS:

SCHEDULE

TIME	APPOINTMENT

PRIORITIES / GOALS

- ○
- ○
- ○
- ○
- ○
- ○
- ○
- ○
- ○
- ○

NOTES & SCRIBBLES

HABITS – 1 NEW PER MONTH

1.
2.
3.

TODAY I'M GRATEFUL FOR

WEDNESDAY
NOVEMBER 2024

27

TODAY'S PRAYER & FOCUS:

SCHEDULE

TIME	APPOINTMENT

PRIORITIES / GOALS

○
○
○
○
○
○
○
○
○
○

NOTES & SCRIBBLES

HABITS – 1 NEW PER MONTH
1.
2.
3.

TODAY I'M GRATEFUL FOR

28 THURSDAY
NOVEMBER 2024

TODAY'S PRAYER & FOCUS:

SCHEDULE

TIME	APPOINTMENT

PRIORITIES / GOALS

○
○
○
○
○
○
○
○
○
○

NOTES & SCRIBBLES

HABITS – 1 NEW PER MONTH

1.
2.
3.

TODAY I'M GRATEFUL FOR

FRIDAY
NOVEMBER 2024
29

TODAY'S PRAYER & FOCUS:

SCHEDULE

TIME	APPOINTMENT

PRIORITIES / GOALS

- ○
- ○
- ○
- ○
- ○
- ○
- ○
- ○
- ○
- ○

NOTES & SCRIBBLES

HABITS – 1 NEW PER MONTH
1.
2.
3.

TODAY I'M GRATEFUL FOR

30
SATURDAY
NOVEMBER 2024

TODAY'S PRAYER & FOCUS:

SCHEDULE

TIME	APPOINTMENT

PRIORITIES / GOALS

- ○
- ○
- ○
- ○
- ○
- ○
- ○
- ○
- ○
- ○

NOTES & SCRIBBLES

HABITS — 1 NEW PER MONTH

1.
2.
3.

TODAY I'M GRATEFUL FOR

SUNDAY
DECEMBER 2024

1

TODAY'S PRAYER & FOCUS:

SCHEDULE

TIME	APPOINTMENT

PRIORITIES / GOALS

- ○
- ○
- ○
- ○
- ○
- ○
- ○
- ○
- ○

NOTES & SCRIBBLES

HABITS – 1 NEW PER MONTH
1.
2.
3.

TODAY I'M GRATEFUL FOR

NOVEMBER 2024 INCOME TRACKER

DATE	INCOME	CATEGORY	AMOUNT
TOTAL			

NOVEMBER 2024 EXPENSE TRACKER

DATE	EXPENSE	CATEGORY	AMOUNT
TOTAL			

NOVEMBER 2024 SAVINGS TRACKER

SAVING FOR: _____   GOAL AMOUNT: _____

DATE	NOTES	AMOUNT	BALANCE
TOTAL			

MONTHLY PROGRESS - NOVEMBER 2024

I HAVE ACHIEVED...

I AM THANKFUL...

I'D LIKE TO IMPROVE...

HOW I WILL CELEBRATE WHAT I DID WELL...

DECEMBER

MONDAY	TUESDAY	WEDNESDAY	THURSDAY
2	3	4	5
9	10	11	12
16	17	18	19
23	24	25	26
30	31		

GOALS

2024

FRIDAY	SATURDAY	SUNDAY	NOTES
6	7	8	
13	14	15	
20	21	22	
27	28	29	

NOTES

MASTER SUCCESS ACTIONS
DECEMBER 2024

List 4 life areas and your goals to focus on this month:

1.

2.

3.

4.

Use this master task list for the big action steps you will commit to do this month. They will accomplish the goals you set to improve your life in the 4 areas of focus. Your daily tasks will be the small steps to accomplish these bigger steps.

DONE	SUCCESS ACTIONS

NOTES

WEEKLY PLANNER

QUOTE OF THE WEEK:

MONDAY
2

TUESDAY
3

WEDNESDAY
4

THURSDAY
5

FRIDAY
6

SATURDAY
7

SUNDAY
8

SUCCESS FOCUS:

PRIORITIES / GOALS

- ○
- ○
- ○
- ○
- ○
- ○
- ○
- ○
- ○

NOTES

DECEMBER 2 – 8, 2024

	BREAKFAST	LUNCH	DINNER	SNACKS
M				
T				
W				
T				
F				
S				
S				

SHOPPING LIST:

NOTES

MONDAY
DECEMBER 2024

2

TODAY'S PRAYER & FOCUS:

SCHEDULE

TIME	APPOINTMENT

PRIORITIES / GOALS

- ○
- ○
- ○
- ○
- ○
- ○
- ○
- ○
- ○
- ○

NOTES & SCRIBBLES

HABITS – 1 NEW PER MONTH
1.
2.
3.

TODAY I'M GRATEFUL FOR

3

TUESDAY
DECEMBER 2024

TODAY'S PRAYER & FOCUS:

SCHEDULE

TIME	APPOINTMENT

PRIORITIES / GOALS

- ○
- ○
- ○
- ○
- ○
- ○
- ○
- ○
- ○
- ○

NOTES & SCRIBBLES

HABITS – 1 NEW PER MONTH

1.
2.
3.

TODAY I'M GRATEFUL FOR

WEDNESDAY
DECEMBER 2024

4

TODAY'S PRAYER & FOCUS:

SCHEDULE

TIME	APPOINTMENT

PRIORITIES / GOALS

- ○
- ○
- ○
- ○
- ○
- ○
- ○
- ○
- ○
- ○

NOTES & SCRIBBLES

HABITS – 1 NEW PER MONTH
1.
2.
3.

TODAY I'M GRATEFUL FOR

5

THURSDAY
DECEMBER 2024

TODAY'S PRAYER & FOCUS:

SCHEDULE

TIME	APPOINTMENT

PRIORITIES / GOALS

- ○
- ○
- ○
- ○
- ○
- ○
- ○
- ○
- ○
- ○

NOTES & SCRIBBLES

HABITS – 1 NEW PER MONTH

1.
2.
3.

TODAY I'M GRATEFUL FOR

FRIDAY
DECEMBER 2024
6

TODAY'S PRAYER & FOCUS:

SCHEDULE

TIME	APPOINTMENT

PRIORITIES / GOALS

- ○
- ○
- ○
- ○
- ○
- ○
- ○
- ○
- ○

NOTES & SCRIBBLES

HABITS – 1 NEW PER MONTH
1.
2.
3.

TODAY I'M GRATEFUL FOR

7

SATURDAY
DECEMBER 2024

TODAY'S PRAYER & FOCUS:

SCHEDULE

TIME	APPOINTMENT

PRIORITIES / GOALS

- ○
- ○
- ○
- ○
- ○
- ○
- ○
- ○
- ○

NOTES & SCRIBBLES

HABITS – 1 NEW PER MONTH

1.
2.
3.

TODAY I'M GRATEFUL FOR

SUNDAY
DECEMBER 2024

8

TODAY'S PRAYER & FOCUS:

SCHEDULE

TIME	APPOINTMENT

PRIORITIES / GOALS

- ○
- ○
- ○
- ○
- ○
- ○
- ○
- ○
- ○
- ○

NOTES & SCRIBBLES

HABITS – 1 NEW PER MONTH
1.
2.
3.

TODAY I'M GRATEFUL FOR

WEEKLY PLANNER

QUOTE OF THE WEEK:

MONDAY
9

TUESDAY
10

WEDNESDAY
11

THURSDAY
12

FRIDAY
13

SATURDAY
14

SUNDAY
15

SUCCESS FOCUS:

PRIORITIES / GOALS

- ○
- ○
- ○
- ○
- ○
- ○
- ○
- ○
- ○

NOTES

DECEMBER 9 – 15, 2024

	BREAKFAST	LUNCH	DINNER	SNACKS
M				
T				
W				
T				
F				
S				
S				

SHOPPING LIST:

NOTES

MONDAY
DECEMBER 2024
9

TODAY'S PRAYER & FOCUS:

SCHEDULE

TIME	APPOINTMENT

PRIORITIES / GOALS

-
-
-
-
-
-
-
-
-
-

NOTES & SCRIBBLES

HABITS – 1 NEW PER MONTH
1.
2.
3.

TODAY I'M GRATEFUL FOR

10 TUESDAY
DECEMBER 2024

TODAY'S PRAYER & FOCUS:

SCHEDULE

TIME	APPOINTMENT

PRIORITIES / GOALS

- ◯
- ◯
- ◯
- ◯
- ◯
- ◯
- ◯
- ◯
- ◯
- ◯

NOTES & SCRIBBLES

HABITS – 1 NEW PER MONTH
1.
2.
3.

TODAY I'M GRATEFUL FOR

WEDNESDAY
DECEMBER 2024 — 11

TODAY'S PRAYER & FOCUS:

SCHEDULE

TIME	APPOINTMENT

PRIORITIES / GOALS

- ◯
- ◯
- ◯
- ◯
- ◯
- ◯
- ◯
- ◯
- ◯
- ◯

NOTES & SCRIBBLES

HABITS – 1 NEW PER MONTH
1.
2.
3.

TODAY I'M GRATEFUL FOR

12

THURSDAY
DECEMBER 2024

TODAY'S PRAYER & FOCUS:

SCHEDULE

TIME	APPOINTMENT

PRIORITIES / GOALS

- ○
- ○
- ○
- ○
- ○
- ○
- ○
- ○
- ○
- ○

NOTES & SCRIBBLES

HABITS – 1 NEW PER MONTH

1.
2.
3.

TODAY I'M GRATEFUL FOR

FRIDAY
DECEMBER 2024
13

TODAY'S PRAYER & FOCUS:

SCHEDULE

TIME	APPOINTMENT

PRIORITIES / GOALS

- ◯
- ◯
- ◯
- ◯
- ◯
- ◯
- ◯
- ◯
- ◯
- ◯

NOTES & SCRIBBLES

HABITS – 1 NEW PER MONTH
1.
2.
3.

TODAY I'M GRATEFUL FOR

14

SATURDAY
DECEMBER 2024

TODAY'S PRAYER & FOCUS:

SCHEDULE

TIME	APPOINTMENT

PRIORITIES / GOALS

- ◯
- ◯
- ◯
- ◯
- ◯
- ◯
- ◯
- ◯
- ◯

NOTES & SCRIBBLES

HABITS – 1 NEW PER MONTH

1.
2.
3.

TODAY I'M GRATEFUL FOR

SUNDAY
DECEMBER 2024   **15**

TODAY'S PRAYER & FOCUS:

SCHEDULE

TIME	APPOINTMENT

PRIORITIES / GOALS

- ◯
- ◯
- ◯
- ◯
- ◯
- ◯
- ◯
- ◯
- ◯
- ◯

NOTES & SCRIBBLES

HABITS – 1 NEW PER MONTH
1.
2.
3.

TODAY I'M GRATEFUL FOR

WEEKLY PLANNER

QUOTE OF THE WEEK:

MONDAY 16	**PRIORITIES / GOALS**
TUESDAY 17	○ ○ ○ ○
WEDNESDAY 18	○ ○
THURSDAY 19	○ ○ ○
FRIDAY 20	○
SATURDAY 21	**NOTES**
SUNDAY 22	

SUCCESS FOCUS:

DECEMBER 16 – 22, 2024

	BREAKFAST	LUNCH	DINNER	SNACKS
M				
T				
W				
T				
F				
S				
S				

SHOPPING LIST:

NOTES

MONDAY
DECEMBER 2024
16

TODAY'S PRAYER & FOCUS:

SCHEDULE

TIME	APPOINTMENT

PRIORITIES / GOALS

- ○
- ○
- ○
- ○
- ○
- ○
- ○
- ○
- ○
- ○

NOTES & SCRIBBLES

HABITS – 1 NEW PER MONTH
1.
2.
3.

TODAY I'M GRATEFUL FOR

17

TUESDAY
DECEMBER 2024

TODAY'S PRAYER & FOCUS:

SCHEDULE

TIME	APPOINTMENT

PRIORITIES / GOALS

- ◯
- ◯
- ◯
- ◯
- ◯
- ◯
- ◯
- ◯
- ◯
- ◯

NOTES & SCRIBBLES

HABITS – 1 NEW PER MONTH

1.
2.
3.

TODAY I'M GRATEFUL FOR

WEDNESDAY
DECEMBER 2024
18

TODAY'S PRAYER & FOCUS:

SCHEDULE

TIME	APPOINTMENT

PRIORITIES / GOALS

- ◯
- ◯
- ◯
- ◯
- ◯
- ◯
- ◯
- ◯
- ◯
- ◯

NOTES & SCRIBBLES

HABITS – 1 NEW PER MONTH

1.
2.
3.

TODAY I'M GRATEFUL FOR

19

THURSDAY
DECEMBER 2024

TODAY'S PRAYER & FOCUS:

SCHEDULE

TIME	APPOINTMENT

PRIORITIES / GOALS

- ○
- ○
- ○
- ○
- ○
- ○
- ○
- ○
- ○

NOTES & SCRIBBLES

HABITS – 1 NEW PER MONTH

1.
2.
3.

TODAY I'M GRATEFUL FOR

FRIDAY
DECEMBER 2024 **20**

TODAY'S PRAYER & FOCUS:

SCHEDULE

TIME	APPOINTMENT

PRIORITIES / GOALS

- ○
- ○
- ○
- ○
- ○
- ○
- ○
- ○
- ○
- ○

NOTES & SCRIBBLES

HABITS – 1 NEW PER MONTH
1.
2.
3.

TODAY I'M GRATEFUL FOR

21

SATURDAY
DECEMBER 2024

TODAY'S PRAYER & FOCUS:

SCHEDULE

TIME	APPOINTMENT

PRIORITIES / GOALS

- ◯
- ◯
- ◯
- ◯
- ◯
- ◯
- ◯
- ◯
- ◯
- ◯

NOTES & SCRIBBLES

HABITS – 1 NEW PER MONTH

1.
2.
3.

TODAY I'M GRATEFUL FOR

SUNDAY
DECEMBER 2024
22

TODAY'S PRAYER & FOCUS:

SCHEDULE

TIME	APPOINTMENT

PRIORITIES / GOALS

- ○
- ○
- ○
- ○
- ○
- ○
- ○
- ○
- ○

NOTES & SCRIBBLES

HABITS – 1 NEW PER MONTH
1.
2.
3.

TODAY I'M GRATEFUL FOR

WEEKLY PLANNER

QUOTE OF THE WEEK:

| MONDAY 23 |
| TUESDAY 24 |
| WEDNESDAY 25 |
| THURSDAY 26 |
| FRIDAY 27 |
| SATURDAY 28 |
| SUNDAY 29 |

PRIORITIES / GOALS

○
○
○
○
○
○
○
○
○
○

NOTES

SUCCESS FOCUS:

DECEMBER 23 – 29, 2024

	BREAKFAST	LUNCH	DINNER	SNACKS
M				
T				
W				
T				
F				
S				
S				

SHOPPING LIST:

NOTES

MONDAY
DECEMBER 2024 **23**

TODAY'S PRAYER & FOCUS:

SCHEDULE

TIME	APPOINTMENT

PRIORITIES / GOALS

- ◯
- ◯
- ◯
- ◯
- ◯
- ◯
- ◯
- ◯
- ◯
- ◯

NOTES & SCRIBBLES

HABITS – 1 NEW PER MONTH
1.
2.
3.

TODAY I'M GRATEFUL FOR

24

TUESDAY
DECEMBER 2024

TODAY'S PRAYER & FOCUS:

SCHEDULE

TIME	APPOINTMENT

PRIORITIES / GOALS

○
○
○
○
○
○
○
○
○
○

NOTES & SCRIBBLES

HABITS – 1 NEW PER MONTH
1.
2.
3.

TODAY I'M GRATEFUL FOR

WEDNESDAY
DECEMBER 2024
25

TODAY'S PRAYER & FOCUS:

SCHEDULE

TIME	APPOINTMENT

PRIORITIES / GOALS

- ○
- ○
- ○
- ○
- ○
- ○
- ○
- ○
- ○
- ○

NOTES & SCRIBBLES

HABITS – 1 NEW PER MONTH

1.
2.
3.

TODAY I'M GRATEFUL FOR

26
THURSDAY
DECEMBER 2024

TODAY'S PRAYER & FOCUS:

SCHEDULE

TIME	APPOINTMENT

PRIORITIES / GOALS

- ○
- ○
- ○
- ○
- ○
- ○
- ○
- ○
- ○
- ○

NOTES & SCRIBBLES

HABITS – 1 NEW PER MONTH
1.
2.
3.

TODAY I'M GRATEFUL FOR

FRIDAY
DECEMBER 2024
27

TODAY'S PRAYER & FOCUS:

SCHEDULE

TIME	APPOINTMENT

PRIORITIES / GOALS

- ◯
- ◯
- ◯
- ◯
- ◯
- ◯
- ◯
- ◯
- ◯
- ◯

NOTES & SCRIBBLES

HABITS – 1 NEW PER MONTH
1.
2.
3.

TODAY I'M GRATEFUL FOR

28

SATURDAY
DECEMBER 2024

TODAY'S PRAYER & FOCUS:

SCHEDULE

TIME	APPOINTMENT

PRIORITIES / GOALS

○
○
○
○
○
○
○
○
○
○

NOTES & SCRIBBLES

HABITS – 1 NEW PER MONTH

1.
2.
3.

TODAY I'M GRATEFUL FOR

SUNDAY
DECEMBER 2024
29

TODAY'S PRAYER & FOCUS:

SCHEDULE

TIME	APPOINTMENT

PRIORITIES / GOALS

- ○
- ○
- ○
- ○
- ○
- ○
- ○
- ○
- ○
- ○

NOTES & SCRIBBLES

HABITS – 1 NEW PER MONTH
1.
2.
3.

TODAY I'M GRATEFUL FOR

WEEKLY PLANNER

QUOTE OF THE WEEK:

MONDAY
30

TUESDAY
31

WEDNESDAY
1

THURSDAY
2

FRIDAY
3

SATURDAY
4

SUNDAY
5

SUCCESS FOCUS:

PRIORITIES / GOALS

○
○
○
○
○
○
○
○
○

NOTES

DECEMBER 30, 2024 – JANUARY 5, 2025

	BREAKFAST	LUNCH	DINNER	SNACKS
M				
T				
W				
T				
F				
S				
S				

SHOPPING LIST:

NOTES

MONDAY
DECEMBER 2024 — 30

TODAY'S PRAYER & FOCUS:

SCHEDULE

TIME	APPOINTMENT

PRIORITIES / GOALS

- ○
- ○
- ○
- ○
- ○
- ○
- ○
- ○
- ○
- ○

NOTES & SCRIBBLES

HABITS – 1 NEW PER MONTH
1.
2.
3.

TODAY I'M GRATEFUL FOR

31

TUESDAY
DECEMBER 2024

TODAY'S PRAYER & FOCUS:

SCHEDULE

TIME	APPOINTMENT

PRIORITIES / GOALS

○
○
○
○
○
○
○
○
○
○

NOTES & SCRIBBLES

HABITS – 1 NEW PER MONTH

1.
2.
3.

TODAY I'M GRATEFUL FOR

WEDNESDAY
JANUARY 2025

1

TODAY'S PRAYER & FOCUS:

SCHEDULE

TIME	APPOINTMENT

PRIORITIES / GOALS

- ◯
- ◯
- ◯
- ◯
- ◯
- ◯
- ◯
- ◯
- ◯
- ◯

NOTES & SCRIBBLES

HABITS – 1 NEW PER MONTH

1.
2.
3.

TODAY I'M GRATEFUL FOR

2

THURSDAY
JANUARY 2025

TODAY'S PRAYER & FOCUS:

SCHEDULE

TIME	APPOINTMENT

PRIORITIES / GOALS

- ◯
- ◯
- ◯
- ◯
- ◯
- ◯
- ◯
- ◯
- ◯
- ◯

NOTES & SCRIBBLES

HABITS – 1 NEW PER MONTH

1.
2.
3.

TODAY I'M GRATEFUL FOR

FRIDAY
JANUARY 2025

3

TODAY'S PRAYER & FOCUS:

SCHEDULE

TIME	APPOINTMENT

PRIORITIES / GOALS

- ◯
- ◯
- ◯
- ◯
- ◯
- ◯
- ◯
- ◯
- ◯
- ◯

NOTES & SCRIBBLES

HABITS – 1 NEW PER MONTH

1.
2.
3.

TODAY I'M GRATEFUL FOR

4

SATURDAY
JANUARY 2025

TODAY'S PRAYER & FOCUS:

SCHEDULE

TIME	APPOINTMENT

PRIORITIES / GOALS

- ○
- ○
- ○
- ○
- ○
- ○
- ○
- ○
- ○
- ○

NOTES & SCRIBBLES

HABITS – 1 NEW PER MONTH

1.
2.
3.

TODAY I'M GRATEFUL FOR

SUNDAY
JANUARY 2025

5

TODAY'S PRAYER & FOCUS:

SCHEDULE

TIME	APPOINTMENT

PRIORITIES / GOALS

- ○
- ○
- ○
- ○
- ○
- ○
- ○
- ○
- ○
- ○

NOTES & SCRIBBLES

HABITS – 1 NEW PER MONTH
1.
2.
3.

TODAY I'M GRATEFUL FOR

DECEMBER 2024 INCOME TRACKER

DATE	INCOME	CATEGORY	AMOUNT
TOTAL			

DECEMBER 2024 EXPENSE TRACKER

DATE	EXPENSE	CATEGORY	AMOUNT
TOTAL			

DECEMBER 2024 SAVINGS TRACKER

SAVING FOR: _____   GOAL AMOUNT: _____

DATE	NOTES	AMOUNT	BALANCE
TOTAL			

MONTHLY PROGRESS - DECEMBER 2024

I HAVE ACHIEVED...

I AM THANKFUL...

I'D LIKE TO IMPROVE...

HOW I WILL CELEBRATE WHAT I DID WELL...

BOOKS TO READ

TITLE	AUTHOR	✓

WISH LIST

PRODUCT	PRICE	STORE

WEBSITE/APP LIST

URL/APP NAME	USERNAME	PASSWORD

GIFTS LIST

TO/FROM	GIFT	THANK YOU

NOTES

NOTES

NOTES

NOTES

NOTES

NOTES

NOTES

NOTES

NOTES

NOTES

NOTES

NOTES

NOTES

NOTES

NOTES

NOTES

NOTES

NOTES

NOTES

NOTES

INDEX

TOPIC	PAGE(S)

INDEX

TOPIC	PAGE(S)

INDEX

TOPIC	PAGE(S)

INDEX

TOPIC	PAGE(S)

www.ingramcontent.com/pod-product-compliance
Lightning Source LLC
Chambersburg PA
CBHW052051220426
43663CB00012B/2521